Copyright© 2023 Line by Lion Publications

ISBN: 978-1-948807-64-7

All rights reserved. No part of this book may be reproduced or used in any manner without written permission of the copyright holder except for use of quotations in a book review.

TO AMY — I KNEW AS SOON AS I SAW THAT JACKET THAT WE WOULD BE FRIENDS. I COULD NOT HAVE PREDICTED, HOWEVER, HOW IMPORTANT YOU WOULD BECOME TO ME. THIS BOOK WOULD NOT EXIST WITHOUT YOUR — ERHEM — GENTLE ENCOURAGEMENT. I LOVE YOU.

IT WAS MORNING IN THE RAINFOREST. THE MACAWS WERE SQUAWKING, THE MONKEYS WERE HOOTING. IT WAS CHEERFUL, AND SUNNY AND LOUD!

All of the noise woke up Gilbert the capybara. Most capybara were relaxed and jolly creatures. But not Gilbert. Gilbert was cranky, and being woken up just made it worse.

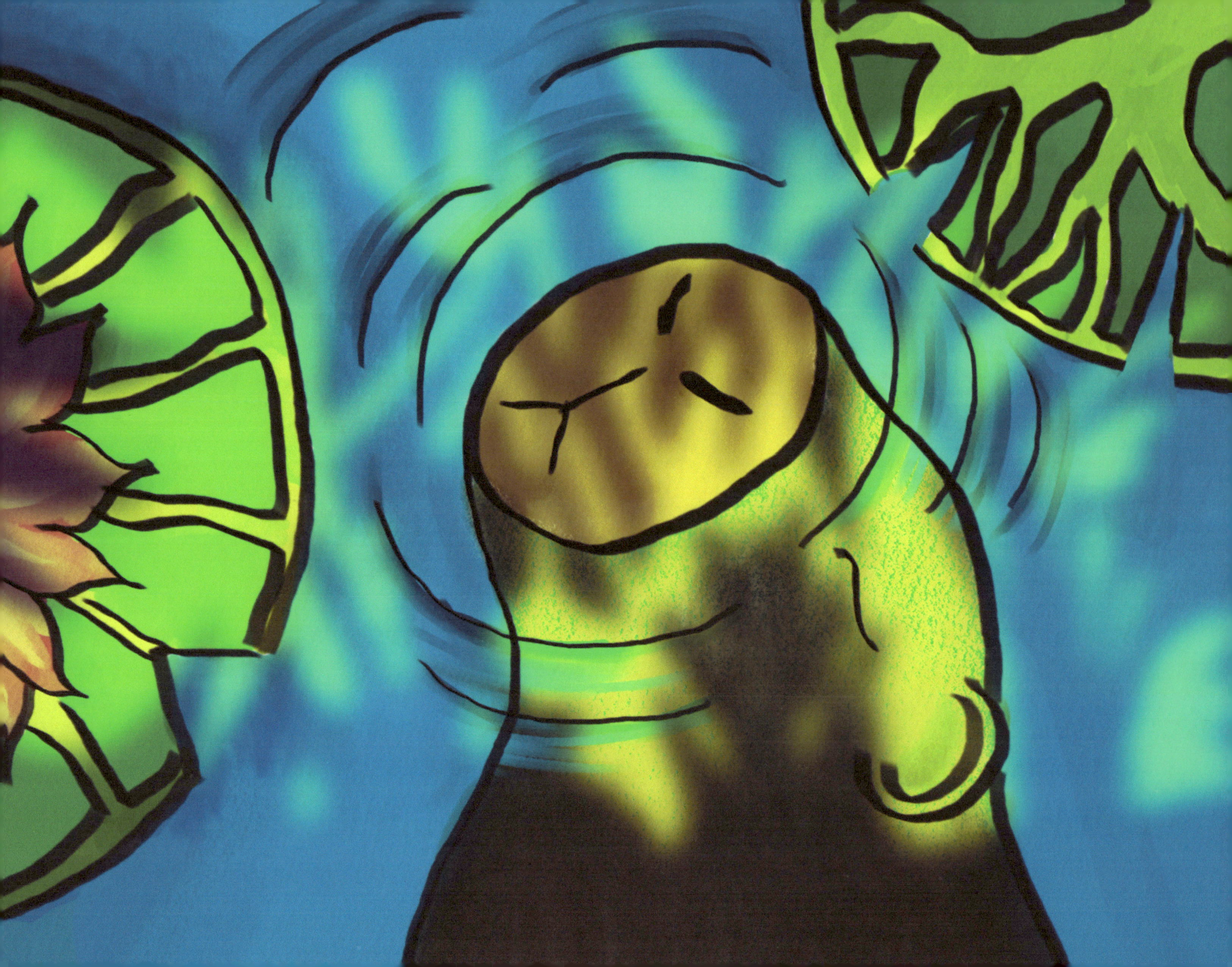

"MAYBE IF I GO INTO THE POND I CAN NAP A BIT" THOUGHT GILBERT CRANKILY. SO, HE SANK INTO THE WATER SO THAT ONLY HIS NOSTRILS STUCK OUT, CLOSED HIS EYES, AND WENT TO SLEEP.

IT WASN'T VERY LONG AT ALL BEFORE GILBERT FELT SOMETHING BUMPING AGAINST HIS CHEEK. HE OPENED ONE EYE SLEEPILY, AND THERE WAS A YOUNG CAIMAN. "EXCUSE ME," SAID THE CAIMAN. "MY NAME IS NIGEL, AND I WAS WONDERING IF YOU'D LIKE TO BE MY FRIEND."

"NO," SAID GILBERT. HE GOT OUT OF THE POND AND SHOOK TO GET THE WATER OFF OF HIS FUR. HE WIGGLED FIRST ONE LEG, AND THEN THE OTHER. NIGEL FOLLOWED. "BUT WHY?" HE ASKED.

"Well," Gilbert replied, "if you were my friend, you'd expect me to be happy all of the time. I don't want to have to be happy all of the time." "No I wouldn't," said Nigel. "If I were your friend, I'd be your friend no matter what kind of mood you were in."

Gilbert walked up to the top of the hill where there was a sunny spot. He hoped that Nigel would stay by the water, but instead he walked alongside Gilbert, scurrying on his short legs. "But, if I were your friend, you'd want me to chatter all of the time. I don't like chattering all of the time. It makes me cranky."

Gilbert laid down. He felt a gentle tugging on his fur as Nigel climbed up to lay on top of his head. "No, I wouldn't," Nigel said. "Sometimes, we could just spend time quietly together like we are now. See? This is nice." Gilbert had to agree that it was nice, but he was still cranky.

Gilbert thought for a bit about what Nigel was saying, but mostly he just enjoyed the sun. "So, can we be friends?" asked Nigel. Gilbert sighed. "No," he said. He got up and walked over to some tall grass. Nigel hitched a ride on his back.

Nigel slid off of Gilbert's back. "But why?" he asked. "Because if we were friends, you'd expect me to be just like you," Gilbert said. "And maybe I don't want to be like you." Gilbert pulled up a tuft of grass by the roots. There were some worms on the roots. He shook them off.

Nigel ran up and ate the worms. Gilbert thought that was gross. "No, I wouldn't" Nigel said after he'd swallowed his snack. "I'd want you to be like you! Celebrating differences is one of the best parts of being friends."

Gilbert looked over at the other capybara, snuggling and wrestling in the grass. He didn't like snuggling or wrestling. They made him cranky. "But if we were friends, you'd want us to be together all of the time."

Nigel ran a couple of steps chasing after a beetle as it flew by. After a minute or so, he came back. "No, I wouldn't," he said. "You could do your thing, and I could do mine, and when we came back together we could share stories! So, what do you say; do you want to be friends?"

GILBERT NIBBLED A FLOWER SLOWLY AS HE CONSIDERED WHAT NIGEL SAID. "I GUESS I COULD DO THAT," HE SAID AT LAST, "BUT I'M GOING TO BE CRANKY ABOUT IT." "I CAN LIVE WITH THAT!" SAID NIGEL EXCITEDLY.

ALSO BY LINE BY LION P:UBLICATIONS

www.ingramcontent.com/pod-product-compliance
Lightning Source LLC
Chambersburg PA
CBHW041915230426
43673CB00016B/415